# FATHER DAMIEN

by Pam Brown

**Picture Credits**
Bob Abraham: 14, 25, 28, 40, 49, 57; APA Photo Agency, Singapore: 29 (both), 44;
Mary Evans Picture Library: 8 (top), 34, 35; Hawaiian Tourist Board: 4, 6, 13, 17, 21,
23, 32 (both), 56; Leprosy Mission: 59, 60, 61, 62 (top), 63 (both); LEPRA: 58; The
Picpus Fathers, Louvain: 11, 18, 31, 37, 42, 43, 47, 53, 55; Ann Ronan Picture Library:
8 (bottom), 9; United Society for the Propagation of the Faith: 26 (both), 62. We have
been unable to trace the copyright holder of the pictures on page 7 and would welcome
any information that would enable us to do so. Maps drawn by Geoffrey Pleasance.

Our special thanks go to the Picpus Fathers in Louvain for their support and for
supplying the pictures, without which this book would not have been possible. The
Damiaanmuseum in Tremeloo has many items connected with Damien and his life.

*To Emily*

Published in Great Britain in 1987 by
Exley Publications Ltd
16 Chalk Hill, Watford, Herts WD1 4BN, United Kingdom.
Reprinted 1989

**British Library Cataloguing in Publication Data**
Brown, Pam
       Father Damien. —— (People who have helped the world).
     1.  Damien, *Father.*
     2   Missionaries — Hawaii — Biography — Juvenile literature.
     3.  Missionaries — Belgium — Biography — Juvenile literature.
     I.  Title.
     II. Series.
     610'.92'4     BX4705.D25

**ISBN 1-85015-084-2**

An abridged version of this title, with a reading level of 8-9 years,
is available from LDA, Duke Street, Wisbech, Cambs PE13 2AE.

**Series conceived and edited by Helen Exley.**
Picture research: Diana Briscoe.
Research: Margaret Montgomery.
Typeset by Brush Off Studios, St Albans, Herts.
Printed and bound in Hungary.

# FATHER DAMIEN

*The man who lived and died
for the victims of leprosy*

**Pam Brown**

**≣EXLEY**

# Going to Molokai

You are standing huddled against your mother in a driving, hammering rain that has soaked you both to the skin. She has a tight hold on your hand, but she is not looking at you, or speaking to you. She is staring through the curtain of rain out to sea, like everyone else in the sodden little group on the beach. They all have bundles, but they have long since given up trying to keep them dry. Yours lies at your feet, a roll of palm-leaf matting that holds everything that you possess in the world. You are shivering, not only because you are cold, but also because you are very, very frightened.

Only a week ago the government inspector came to your village with a doctor, who examined you and all your family and spoke very seriously to your mother. She began to cry and everyone in the house – your father, your sisters, your grandmother and your uncle – tried to explain to the doctor that the yellow marks on your arms and the lump on your ear were nothing bad. But he took no notice of them and put down your name, and your mother's, on a piece of printed paper.

After that it was all muddle and crying, until now here you both are, waiting on the stony beach for the boat that is to take you to the island of Molokai, to the leper settlement on the isolated peninsula – the place you have heard called Makandu, which means The Given Grave.

Your father has come with you, but only to say

*ALL LEPERS ARE REQUIRED TO REPORT THEMSELVES TO THE GOVERNMENT HEALTH AUTHORITIES WITHIN FOURTEEN DAYS FROM THIS DATE FOR INSPECTION AND FINAL BANISHMENT TO MOLOKAI.*

*Local notice at the time, in Hawaii*

*A coasting schooner moored off a Hawaiian island, of the kind the leprosy victims would have sailed in.*

goodbye. He is fit and well and though, as you lay in bed, you had heard him trying to persuade your mother to let him go with you both, you know that he cannot come. There are too many people who need him at home.

Other people from your village have been sent to the lonely peninsula on Molokai. Your mother has told you that there will be friends waiting when you land, but all you can think of are the stories you have heard; that no one comes back from Makandu. You look at the other people on the beach, some with missing fingers or open wounds. You know that you will become as ill as they are. And you know that once aboard the boat you will never see your family or friends again.

Now a sigh murmurs through the waiting

people. You look beyond them and see, coming steadily closer, the boat. It looms out of the rain like a shadowy sea monster. A wail starts up all along the beach and people cling to each other ... while the armed police, who have stood at some distance, move closer, guns at the ready.

It is time to go.

## How it was

That child's experience is a terrible thing even to imagine, but about a hundred years ago it happened to many, many people. Today, that same beach is busy with happy tourists, and Molokai is just another Hawaiian island where people go to enjoy the sun and scenery. The once-feared "leper colony" is simply a place for those tourists to visit. Leprosy itself has another name – Hansen's Disease – and can be treated and cured.

People who have the illness are not called "lepers" any more. They are called "leprosy sufferers" or simply "people with leprosy." We now know that people who are ill with leprosy are just like you or me, and that leprosy is just another curable disease. It is not even very catching.

But, when people like the little child and its mother were sent to Molokai, there was no treatment and no cure. Everyone believed it to be the most fearsome and infectious disease in the world. Since biblical times, "leper" had meant something dark and dreadful.

Neglected and untreated, it had a terrible effect on its victims, often making them hideously ugly and deformed. Healthy people were terrified of catching it and sent anyone suspected of having it as far away as possible. If you go into very old churches you may see "squints" – little slit windows that allowed the "lepers" to see the altar without entering the building.

No one knows how long the illness has existed. In the Middle Ages, the word "leper" filled everyone with terror. People who had leprosy had the funeral service said over them, just as if they were already dead. They were given a bell or a

*Leprosy sufferer with physician.*

*"Leper" with bell.*

*"And the leper in whom the plague is, his clothes shall be rent, and the hair of his head shall go loose, and he shall cover his upper lip, and shall cry unclean, unclean.*
*LEVITICUS XIII, 45*

7

Above:
Thirteenth century
engraving of a "leper" with
begging bowl to warn he was
"unclean." During this
period leprosy was at its
worst: one in four people in
Europe had leprosy. It
thrived where people were
poor, badly fed and dirty.

Right:
"Room for the Leper!
Room!" An illustration by
Nathaniel Willis in the
1870s, when Father Damien
had just started his work
with the leprosy sufferers on
Molokai.

*"Lepers" begging on the roadside in Morocco in 1887. They were confined to a village outside the city walls.*

rattle to warn everyone to keep away and were sent off to live as best they could. Some monasteries built places where they could find shelter, but most lived out a lonely and desperate life. It is especially sad to realize that many of them had not got leprosy at all, but only skin troubles that frightened other people.

Despite medical advances over the centuries the old, old fear was still there. People sent to Molokai were still outcasts, and the same mistakes were still being made. It was a terrible place.

But just over one hundred years ago, one brave and good man was to help change life for everyone with leprosy, not only on Molokai, but all over the world.

His name was Damien.

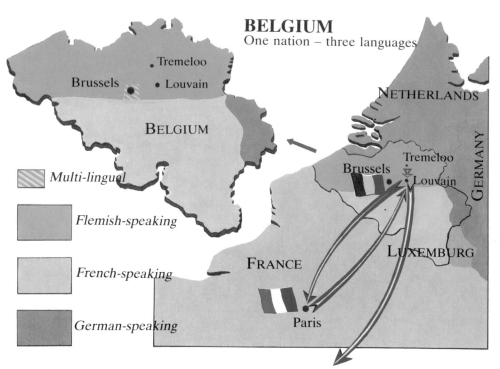

# BELGIUM
One nation – three languages

- Tremeloo
- Brussels
- Louvain

BELGIUM

*Multi-lingual*

*Flemish-speaking*

*French-speaking*

*German-speaking*

NETHERLANDS

Tremeloo

Brussels
Louvain

LUXEMBURG

FRANCE

Paris

GERMANY

*Belgium only became a separate kingdom in 1830, which explains the different languages spoken in its various regions. It was previously divided between France and the Netherlands.*

## Jef becomes Damien

Josef de Veuster-Wouters was born in Tremeloo in Belgium on January 3rd, 1840. He grew up a cheerful, ordinary boy, known to everyone as Jef. He lived a happy life at home, often helping the local builder, Janneke Roef. He learnt carpentry and did all manner of odd jobs for him. Jef had no idea how much he was to need those skills in the years ahead.

His family was solid, respectable and Flemish. Two of his sisters had become nuns and one brother had entered a religious order and was now called Father Pamphile. Jef's father wanted him to go into business and build a successful career for himself.

Businessmen had to know French. In Jef's part of Belgium everyone spoke Flemish so, when he was in his teens, he was sent off to study in the French-speaking part of the country. At first the local students mocked him as a country boy and Flemish-speaking, but Jef had a handy pair of fists and soon knocked a little sense into them.

He was not exceptionally clever, but he was determined and, by making a great effort, he became fluent in French in a surprisingly short time.

By the age of eighteen, Jef had made friends and was making good progress in his studies, but he felt restless and miserable. He was becoming more and more certain that he did not want to go into business, but would far rather be a priest. He decided to join the Sacred Heart or "Picpus" Fathers, like his brother Pamphile.

Now came the difficult part. He hated to disappoint his parents, because he knew how they had had to struggle and save to send him to college, but when he told them what he wanted to do, they understood. They knew he had thought about it for a long time, and all they wanted was for him to be happy.

So Jef went off to Louvain in 1859; he entered the Order and took the name of Damien. With no knowledge of Latin, he could not study for the priesthood as he had hoped, but he was accepted as an ordinary Lay Brother.

He was a very fit, strong young man and his carpentry and building experience soon came in useful. A new chapel was being built and a tall chimney stood in the way. It looked very dangerous indeed and none of the local workmen would touch it. Damien clambered up the ladders and, perched high above the flabbergasted onlookers, got down to the job of dismantling it, brick by brick.

His determination did not stop at chimneys. He got Pamphile to teach him Latin in any spare moments they could find – and soon made such progress that his superiors could not help but be impressed. After six months they allowed him to begin to study for the priesthood.

Long after, people were to say that Damien was an ignorant peasant, but that was never true. Although he was not a brilliant scholar, he already spoke two languages. Then in 1860 he was sent to Paris to learn Latin, Greek and Philosophy.

After that he went back to Louvain to study

*Damien in 1863 when he was 23 years old. He was a Brother with the Sacred Heart Fathers, but had not yet been ordained a priest.*

Theology. He did not find all the work easy, but very badly wanted to be a priest.

He also wanted to go out and work in the Pacific islands. When he was twenty-one, a Bishop from Hawaii had given a talk to the students in Paris and had told them he would like to take some young priests back with him. Damien desperately wanted to go, but he was not yet a priest. To make it harder to bear, his brother was one of those chosen. Poor Damien's heart sank, but then came the chance that was to change his life and that of thousands of people.

There was an epidemic of a fever called typhus. Many people had died and, when Pamphile caught it, Damien was terribly worried. Pamphile was very sick indeed and, though at last he began to get better, he was far too weak to make the long journey to the Pacific.

Damien saw his chance. He knew his superior would probably not let him go, so he wrote directly to the Head of his Order, begging him to take him instead of Pamphile, even though he was not yet a priest. The Superior General must have liked this eager, determined – and rather disobedient – young man, because he agreed that he could go with them.

And so it was Damien, not Pamphile, who set sail in November 1863 on the four-month voyage around Cape Horn to the other side of the world, leaving behind all the old familiar things. He was sailing to a life unlike anything he had ever known.

## The island that needed a friend

Turn the pages of the atlas until you find a map of the vast Pacific Ocean. Scattered across it lie chains of islands like bright beads, and with beautiful, magical names. Héréhérétué, Aitutaki, Rarotonga, Arorae, Nukunonu, Kusaie, Nihoa, Oahu, Yap. The explorers who discovered them were bewitched by their beauty, the dazzling fish that flickered among the reefs, the flowers, and the happy, friendly people.

Tragically, the newcomers brought with them most unwelcome gifts – sicknesses, like measles and the common cold, which meant little in Europe, had killed thousands of the islanders.

*A Hawaiian outrigger canoe of the sort that Damien had his adventure in.*

Worst of all, the Chinese who came to work on the islands unknowingly brought with them the most feared disease of all – leprosy. The Hawaiian people called it *Ma'i Pake*, the Chinese Disease.

By 1865 the government of the Hawaiian islands, which lie in the northern Pacific, had become so frightened by the spread of the illness that they decided that everyone who caught it must be sent to an isolated peninsula called Kalaupapa on the north coast of the island of Molokai. That may seem a very cruel thing to do, but in those days no one knew much about leprosy. The only way to stop it spreading seemed to be to keep leprosy sufferers away from healthy people.

What was very wrong however was that no one

*An aerial view of the Kalaupapa peninsula on Molokai where shiploads of people with leprosy were exiled. The cliffs formed an impassable barricade to the other side of the island.*

*Opposite:*
*The Hawaiian group consists of over 20 volcanic islands and atolls. Here are the six main islands including Molokai, which is only 10 miles across from North to South. On the north coast the map shows a bump, which is the peninsula where the leprosy colony was.*

seemed to bother about what happened to the sick people once they were on the island. The old saying, "Out of sight, out of mind" seemed to be true of Molokai.

The first people who landed at Kalaupapa were given a supply of seeds and tools. However, no one realized that, as their hands and feet were rotting away, or twisted and nearly useless, it was quite impossible for them to use the equipment.

The huts they were to live in had been hastily thrown together and were made from branches, leaves and grass. A building called "the hospital" had been put up, but as there were no beds in it, no medicines and no doctor, it could scarcely be thought of as one.

People died, not from the disease, but from starvation. They grew so desperate that they ran wild: fighting, drinking and gambling. The government sent troops to try to restore order, but they were too afraid of catching leprosy to go anywhere near the offenders.

To try to pacify them the government sent out a few cattle, some clothes and food, and a man

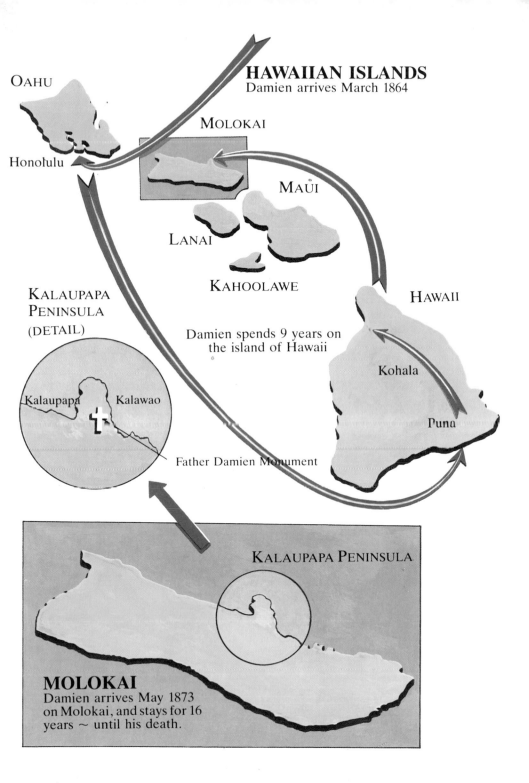

HAWAIIAN ISLANDS
Damien arrives March 1864

OAHU

Honolulu

MOLOKAI

MAUI

LANAI

KAHOOLAWE

HAWAII

Damien spends 9 years on
the island of Hawaii

Kohala

Puna

KALAUPAPA
PENINSULA
(DETAIL)

Kalaupapa        Kalawao

Father Damien Monument

KALAUPAPA PENINSULA

MOLOKAI
Damien arrives May 1873
on Molokai, and stays for 16
years ~ until his death.

to take charge. He stayed for only a few weeks and then went back to Honolulu, leaving the people convinced that no one cared at all what happened to them.

Everyone on the other islands knew what it was like there: even the name "Molokai" made them afraid. The sick people, who were wrenched away from their homes and families and friends, were sometimes so mad with grief and despair that they fought not to be unloaded into the rowing boats that ferried them from the ship to the landing stage at Kalaupapa. If they did fight, they were thrown overboard to struggle to shore as best they could, or to drown. Those who were landed by boat often had their few belongings stolen almost at once. They found themselves in a world where there seemed no hope at all. They were told "Aole kanawai ma keia wahi" (In this place, there is no law).

You can imagine how the child and its mother must have felt when they were bundled on to the beach and led away over the rough road to Kalawao, with its filthy windowless huts and its population of desperately sick people, knowing there was never to be any escape.

They did not know that on the other side of the world Damien was setting sail and that he would eventually come to the island to be their friend and helper.

## Hawaii at last

If you were told that you were going to the Hawaiian islands I expect you would be very excited. You could find out a great deal about them from television, books and glossy photographs, and you would know that they were only a few hours away by plane from your home.

In 1863, when Damien set out, it was nothing like that. Damien was excited, but all he knew about his new home was from what people told him and from books. It seemed an immense distance away and the journey took four months by sailing ship. They arrived in March, 1864.

*"You could not wish for better people; gentle, pleasant-mannered, exceedingly tender-hearted, they neither seek to amass riches, or live in luxury, or dress much, but are most hospitable, and ready to deprive themselves even of necessities in order to supply your every want if you have to ask a night's shelter from them..."*

Father Damien, in a letter to his brother, Father Pamphile, dated August 8, 1864.

They were to land at Honolulu, on Oahu. Even then it was a fine city, with a busy port and very grand buildings. But the islands had not altered as much as they have today.

*A grove of coconut palms; just one of the many new plants and trees Damien would have encountered.*

Can you imagine what it must have been like; those first glimpses of the islands rising from the glittering sea, the scent of flowers and leaves drifting across the water? The passengers must have crowded to the ship's rail to watch the coast become clearer and clearer. Perhaps, as they followed the shore line, they saw outrigger canoes come out to greet them, and brown-skinned children swimming like fish in the clear water.

The young men, and the nuns who went with them, were welcomed by the missionaries and soon settled in. Damien at once started to learn his *fifth* language, Kanaka, so that he could speak to the local people in their own tongue. He also had to complete the studies he had kept up on the journey out. Two months after arriving, he was ordained a priest and, a little nervously, was sent off to his very first job, a run-down Mission in Puna, on Hawaii Island.

# Nine years on Hawaii Island

When he arrived the people were friendly and welcoming, but Damien found it all very unlike the life he had lived in Europe. In those days people from the West were very puzzled and bewildered by those who lived a life so different from their own.

Still, he built a house and a church and began his work, calling people to mass not with a bell, but by blowing on a conch shell. The people were kind, but he missed his friends. He was sometimes so lonely that he would trek for miles across difficult country, just for a few hours conversation with another priest. This loneliness was to haunt him all his life.

In March 1865, he heard that Father Clemens who he had met on the ship, was exhausted, as his Mission in Kohala covered two thousand square miles. Damien suggested they swap over. Once there, he heard of an even more remote area, near his Mission, where there were some Christians and set off by canoe to visit them. It capsized in heavy seas; he and the crew only survived by hanging on to the upturned boat and dog-paddling to shore. He was very shaken by the experience but when he wrote home he was very careful to make it sound like an amusing adventure. Damien always kept his letters to his family cheerful, only telling the whole truth to his brother, Pamphile.

As you will have guessed, such a near-catastrophe was not going to deter Damien. He set off again, this time by the dangerous overland route that he had tried to avoid. He rode as far as he could but, when the path got too bad, he was forced to dismount and struggle the rest of the way on foot. It took him four days.

This new area needed a church so, with the help of the local people, Damien set to. Using the skills he had learned as a boy, the building soon took shape. Everyone was astounded by his strength and skill as he manhandled the biggest timbers into place and scrambled about on the roof. They all felt they had to work harder to keep up with him. It was a hard life, but Damien was never happy unless he was busy.

He was learning more about the islands every day. You have probably seen earthquakes and volcanoes on television – they look wonderfully dramatic and exciting. Damien did not find them so. Two weeks of earthquakes caused great devastation in the countryside and villages, and forty of his new-found friends were killed. When later in his life visitors talked to him about the magnificence of volcanic eruptions, he could never share their enthusiasm.

## Goodbye to Kohala

The little villages were widely scattered, which meant long journeys in all kinds of weather. Hawaii is one of the most beautiful places in the world, but it probably did not seem so when Damien was pushing his way through under-growth in slashing rain.

The forests of tree ferns were full of the most beautiful flowers and the dramatic beaches were dotted with the twisted shapes of crumbling black lava. Damien had very little time to consider their beauty and was very thankful indeed when, in October 1869, a young priest called Father Aubert was sent to help him.

Damien scarcely gave him time to get his breath back after his journey, before setting him to work. Damien could never see why others could not work as hard or as long as he himself was able to!

The two men liked each other, but they scarcely ever saw one another as they had to work so many miles apart for most of the time. They were always busy. Life was interesting and went along without too many problems for nearly nine years.

Then in May 1873 Damien and Father Aubert were asked to take part in the celebrations at the consecration of a new church at Wailuku on Maui. While they were there, Bishop Maigret spoke to the young priests who had come, telling them of the terrible conditions on Molokai, and how the people there had begged him to send a priest to be their friend.

*Volcanic eruptions are common on the Hawaiian islands. They're very dramatic and beautiful, but they can cause much suffering for the local people.*

Damien had seen new victims of leprosy rounded up and bullied aboard the ships bound for Molokai and had never forgotten the look of terror and despair on their faces. When the Bishop asked for volunteers, he and another three priests all offered to go at once.

The Bishop was deeply moved. He said he would never send anyone to such a dreadful place unless they were willing to go and he was grateful to them. His idea was that they should take turns on the island, but decided that Damien, fit and strong and capable, should be the first.

The Bishop was leaving to go back to Honolulu almost immediately and his boat, the *Kilauea*, was going to call at the leprosy peninsula on

Molokai on the way, to land a cargo of cattle and a group of fifty leprosy sufferers, so Damien could go with them.

Hastily Damien said goodbye to his friends and went aboard, his head spinning a little at the sudden change in his life. He thought that he would take a look around the settlement and see what needed to be done, never dreaming that he would never see Kohala again. He was then 33 years old.

## The world of Molokai

At last the ship dropped anchor off the unfamiliar shore near Kalaupapa village. Towering green cliffs, ribboned with waterfalls, plunged down to the boulder-strewn beaches. To the frightened passengers they seemed like impassable prison walls, shutting them off from the rest of the island. They knew they would never again be allowed off the peninsula. It was May 11, 1873.

Cargo and people were landed and Damien followed them, the Bishop going with him as far as the beach. Damien had seen leprosy before, but what he saw now horrified him. The people were dirty and disfigured – in many cases the disease was far advanced and their hands and feet were mere stumps. They looked less like men and women than terrible ghosts.

As the breakers roared up the beach behind them, the Bishop spoke to the little crowd, telling them that this was the priest they had asked for, and that Father Damien would stay and look after them. Then he said goodbye to Damien. Dropping his voice, he told him to take great care, then turned and went back to the boat that was waiting for him in the surf.

As the ship moved away, Damien felt horror and loneliness sweep over him. His previous work had been hard, but he could see at a glance that these people would need far more help. He felt that he had neither the skills nor the knowledge needed for such a job. But he decided to tackle things a day at a time. After all, he was better than nothing!

His first sight of the leper village of Kalawao at the foot of the cliffs stunned him. It was far worse than anything he had imagined. As he looked around him, he realized that any idea of finding an abandoned hut to sleep in must be forgotten. They were windowless and dark, filthy and stinking.

The islanders were not like the cheerful, friendly, laughing people he had left behind. Misery and fear had made them suspicious of strangers. They did not believe that he would stay, and they stared at him with blank eyes, or with real anger. Damien knew that it would do no good to rush them. He must take things very quietly, letting them see that he really did want to help them.

A little chapel stood abandoned in the middle of the tangle of huts they called the village. Damien made himself a broom of palm leaves and began to sweep the floor. There were holes in the walls and litter scattered everywhere. Damien cleared away the debris and filled in the holes, quietly busy.

*The original landing beach on the Kalaupapa peninsula, Molokai.*

Gradually people came to watch, though no-one offered to help. Damien noted that although many people were badly affected by the leprosy, some showed scarcely any marks of it at all. This new priest seemed to them a very ordinary sort of man, still young, rather good-looking, and not at all bothered by their appearance. And kind – not at all like officials or inspectors.

A woman brought him some fruit on a leaf and Damien took it from her. He smiled and thanked her in Kanaka. They stared. He spoke their language and he knew the correct forms of greeting!

Someone brought in a spray of flowers and put them on the altar. Damien heaved a hidden sigh of relief – it looked as though they would, after all, accept him as their friend.

He raised his eyes to the frighteningly disfigured group that stood near the door and resolved there and then that, however terrible their appearance, he would never ever allow them to see any sign of revulsion on his face. They had enough to bear, and it would hurt them too deeply. Somehow he must hide his feelings and look through the ugliness to the person inside.

## A waking nightmare

Damien found that one of the hardest things to bear as he explored the village was the appalling smell of the huts, the people and the loathsome graveyard. Luckily he had with him something that would solve the problem. From then on he marched around the island puffing on his pipe, behind a cloud of overpoweringly strong-smelling tobacco.

At the end of the first day he lay down to sleep under a pandanus tree, which was to be his bed until he had managed to build himself a little house. It had all happened so suddenly that it still did not seem quite real, but he was far too tired to stay awake thinking about it. He closed his eyes on stars and trees and village and went to sleep. The next morning when he woke, the nightmare was still there.

The more he explored the peninsula and the two villages, the more horrified he became. Everywhere was dirt and neglect. The people had lost all pride and any hope of things ever getting better. How could even the best of men and women fight the dirt when every drop of water had to be carried half a mile with crippled hands and feet? How could they look after their injuries when there were no medicines and no bandages?

*The ruins of an old leprosy settlement at Kalawao. There was no house for Damien; he slept under a pandanus tree on his first night.*

## The task ahead

In the eight years since the colony was first set up, scarcely a thing had been done to make their lives any better. No wonder they were suspicious of Damien. Many had given up any attempt to live a normal life and passed their days and nights in drunkenness and gambling. Some terrorized the weak, stealing the little they had and, far worse, others took orphaned children to live as their slaves, abandoning them when they became too sick and weak to work any more.

"Here there is no law." Damien kept hearing

This African leprosy victim shows how leprosy can damage the hands and feet. Eventually people are unable to walk, dress, cook or care for themselves. In Father Damien's time the complications from infected wounds were horrific and led to death.

One of the main reasons for fear and rejection of leprosy sufferers has always been that leprosy is one of the most disfiguring diseases in the world.

those words as he went around the villages, and they worried him far more than the poverty, sickness and dirt. What could he do? He was fit and strong, but he was alone. All he had was his strength, his common sense and his courage.

And his temper.

It seems a very odd thing for a priest to need, but Damien knew that if he was to bring order, safety and sanity to the settlement, he must act quickly. As he lay trying to sleep he could hear the raucous laughter, the shrieking and shouting as the drunks staggered around the village. Kind words would do no good.

He leapt to his feet and gave chase. If the people of Molokai had expected a meek and mild priest who would allow them to go on in the same old way, they were very much mistaken. Damien roared out of the darkness, wielding his stick.

In the first weeks he smashed the idols which they had used to frighten the ignorant, invaded the huts and rescued the orphaned children, ignoring the protests of their captors. The bullies cowered away from him and, little by little, Damien brought order back to Kalawao.

He was not only angry with the things which were wrong, but he was also worried about the non-Christian customs of the people who still followed their old traditions. He did not understand, much less sympathize with their ways. It would be many years before white people realized that they could learn a lot from those they had once regarded as "savages," "heathens" or "ignorant natives."

For all that, Damien wanted the settlers to have a far better life than the one they had, and they needed someone like him, who could give them back their self-respect.

## Beginnings

What could Damien do? There was so much that needed doing he scarcely knew where to start.

It is not likely nowadays that a solitary priest would be left alone to cope with such difficulties

*"Discoloured patches appear on the skin, especially on the cheeks; and the parts affected lose their feeling. After a time this discolouration covers the entire body; then ulcers begin to open, chiefly at the extremities. The flesh is eaten away, and gives out a fetid odour; even the breath of the leper becomes so foul that the air around is poisoned with it. I have had great difficulty in getting accustomed to such an atmosphere."*
FATHER DAMIEN

*Father Damien never neglected his religious duties as a Catholic priest. This is the interior of St Philomena which he built and later extended.*

but even if he was, he would probably have been given some basic medical training and he would have arrived weighed down with medicines and sterile bandages, surgical instruments, disinfectants and, best of all, a radio to call for help or advice, or even a helicopter to fly in blankets or clothing or food supplies. Or a doctor. At any rate, he could speak to his friends.

Damien had nothing. There was no treatment and no cure. There was not even a clean piece of rag to bandage up the sores and injuries.

But he still had his temper.

While he went about his new work he began to bombard the government in Honolulu with letters – asking, pleading, demanding the basic things he needed. He needed *everything*. This was the start of a life-long career as the man on Molokai who always wanted something and would nag and nag until he got it. Or so the officials felt. While he waited for answers, he did what he could with what lay to hand.

There was no judge or policeman, no teacher, no doctor or nurse, no expert on building or farming or anything else on the peninsula. Damien had to be all these, on his own. He settled arguments, cleaned and bandaged wounds, repaired the hospital and the church – all in addition to his duties as a priest. These took up to two hours each day and throughout all the crises Damien – *Father Damien* – never neglected them.

He had always worked twice as hard as everyone else. Now he worked even harder. He got some of the fitter men to clear little patches of land and plant sweet potatoes. That not only gave them something to do and to think about, but added to their food supply. Their crops were so good they were able to sell the surplus and make a little money to spend on things they needed. It made them feel they were normal human beings again.

These idols are examples of Hawaiian art. The native people were happy, outgoing and artistic; they worshipped their own gods. Father Damien worked hard to convert the people to Catholicism.

Not everything was so cheerful. People died every day. He nursed them, held their hands, comforted them, but he could not save their lives.

At least they did not die alone.

## Funerals

The first funeral had shocked him. The people of the village had done their best to bury their friends with respect and love, but they could only scrape out shallow graves and wrap the dead in matting. The wild pigs had invaded the graveyard, rooting out the bodies and scattering bones everywhere.

Damien resolved that everyone who died should at least have a decent burial. He made proper coffins and dug deep graves and said the funeral prayers. *In his first six years on Molokai, he was to make most of the coffins and dig graves for one thousand, six hundred people.*

He knew that a tidy, peaceful graveyard, clean bandages and better food were not enough. These people had lived lives without joy, grace or music for so long that it was no wonder they turned to drink and despair. Damien went out of his way to make the church services as beautiful as he knew how. He sent to Honolulu for a bell and made the building bright with fresh flowers.

Few came to his church in the beginning, but gradually more and more ventured in, to be together and sing and to hear what Damien had to say to them. It helped them feel less cut off from the world beyond the sea and the Pali cliffs. Besides, his sermons started "We lepers"; no one else had ever said that before.

## The first help arrives

The newspapers on Oahu and Hawaii had very quickly got to hear of Damien and published articles about his work. The people who read them felt guilty that they had never thought much about Molokai before and organized collections of food and clothes for Damien and his people.

Some of the other church leaders were not at all pleased by the publicity. They thought the praise might go to Damien's head, but Damien was far too busy to think about newspapers. All he was concerned about was the people under his care.

They knew him well now, and they wrote to the Bishop asking that he could stay with them forever. The Bishop replied that nothing definite had been decided yet, but Damien could stay until further notice.

Altogether, he stayed for sixteen years ... until he died.

## Days away

Damien was at first tied to the settlement. He went to Honolulu once, in July 1873 to collect all the good things people had collected for him – and to argue with the government for more help.

> *"He was always willing to leave off work for a time and join the children at their play. On almost any day he could be seen surrounded by romping, laughing youngsters playing tag with them or joining in other childish games. When he joked with the officials, his laugh was always loudest."*
> Charles J. Dutton, from
> *"The Samaritans of Molokai."*

*The Palis of Molokai have
the most beautiful
waterfalls and many types
of flowers. The
Hawaiian islands lie in
the Pacific Ocean,
thousands of miles from
both China in the West, and
California to the East.
Hawaii is very hot and is on
the same latitude as Hong
Kong. In 1898, Hawaii was
annexed by the United
States of America.*

Horrified, the government said he must never leave the peninsula again. He must not even board the boat that called there, to have a word with friends who were aboard.

This was almost too much for Damien to bear. He could not believe it. He, a healthy man, was to be condemned to the life of a "leper." He had never been so hurt or depressed.

Then one night he had a surprise. His old friend, Father Aubert, who seems to have been a little like Damien himself, strode in from the darkness – in disguise! The two old friends talked and laughed the night away and when Aubert left at dawn, Damien felt far more cheerful. Aubert had told him that influential people were doing their very best to get the ban lifted ... and after a very short time it was lifted, early in 1874.

Sometimes Damien longed to talk with someone outside the colony. When he did, he would set off to climb the Pali cliffs, up the rough, dangerous track cut in 1874 that no person with advanced leprosy could manage. The cliffs were thick with undergrowth and dipped into deep, wet ravines. The going was hard, but Damien felt it was worth any struggle to visit his friend the superintendent on the "healthy" side of the island and travel about on the mule that was lent him. He never stayed away very long, for he knew his people needed him, but it lightened his heart and helped him to carry on with his lonely work.

He had long since given up any idea that he would ever be relieved of his job. He did not want to be: but he did wish that his superiors would send *someone* to help him – a doctor, another priest or nuns to take care of the orphans, especially the little girls.

## Peaceful days

Time was passing and Damien had settled in as if he had never lived anywhere else. He had a little one-room hut now, with a thin mattress on the floor and some rather battered furniture. His clothes were growing shabbier with every

*"[In 1873] the huts were small, makeshift affairs of grass or branches or sugarcane leaves, with no ventilation. The wind often blew them to the ground or destroyed them entirely.... The many who had open sores on their feet, could not get about; and these and others in all stages of the putrescent disease lay about in the tiny fetid huts."*
Charles J. Dutton, from "The Samaritans of Molokai."

*"Visiting the sick is my chief daily task. We have to fight their doctors who are generally nothing but sorcerers. In case of sickness idolatrous sacrifices are still in use. All diseases are attributed to mysterious causes. It is very hard to disabuse these poor people of such superstitious notions."*
Father Damien, in a letter to his sister, Sister Pauline, dated July 14, 1872.

passing week. His appearance would not worry people now, but in those days, many people who saw him were shocked. Priests were supposed to be clean and tidy people – a cut above ordinary mortals – but Damien did *not* look very respectable or dignified.

In January 1874, Father André Burgermann had arrived on the "healthy" side of the island. One of his jobs was to build a new church there, but he had no idea how to go about it. So up over the Pali cliffs went Damien with his hammer. Father André looked after the settlement until Damien had organized and built the church – then they changed places again.

It had been a break ... of sorts.

The bandaging of wounds and the funeral services went on – but so did the weddings and the christenings. Happier times had come to Kalawao.

Damien still worried about the children, especially the orphans. He begged the Bishop to send nuns to look after them, but nothing happened. He could not understand why he got so little help, but the Bishop had problems outside Molokai –

*Damien slept under a pandanus tree (or screwpine) when he first came to Molokai. These trees have a peculiar root system that holds its trunk away from the ground, as if on stilts. Often there is quite a large cave inside the roots of an old tree.*

while the Molokai peninsula was now Damien's whole world.

He continued to write to Pamphile, and it is through these letters that we know so much about Damien's work and his deep religious faith.

One of his letters was published in the Order's magazine. Once again, the Superiors and Brothers in Hawaii were indignant – they thought it was a sign of vanity in Damien, who had actually had nothing to do with it. Poor Damien – shabby and tired and overworked – he did not seem very vain to his villagers.

Damien was a deeply religious man and extremely proud of what his Order was achieving in the Hawaiian Islands. Despite his Superiors' refusal of his demands and the jealousy of some of his fellow missionaries, he does not ever seem to have had doubts about his mission. God had called him to minister to the leprosy victims of Molokai, even unto death, and he accepted that call courageously and steadfastly despite all the problems he had to contend with. That, of course, didn't stop him from continually writing, complaining and asking for more for his people.

*An etching, dating from 1889, showing Father Damien's house and church. "I lived a long time under the shelter of a tree, not wishing to sleep under the same roof as the lepers. Later on, the whites of Honolulu having assisted me with their subscriptions, I was able to build myself a hut, sixteen feet long and ten wide, where I am now writing these lines."*

## The fight against Ma'i Pake

Weeks turned to months and months to years. Damien struggled on with native helpers, willing and kindly, but untrained. Mr Williamson, a leprosy sufferer from Europe, also did what he could at the hospital.

Every morning after he had said Mass in his clean, flower-bright church, Damien went on his rounds, finding out how people were and cleaning up their injuries with patient, gentle fingers. Often he had to make an excuse to dash out into the air for a few moments. The huts were in a dreadful state: how could he allow these suffering people to go on living in them?

Damien cared little for comfort or dignity for himself – all he wanted was care for his people. That was hard for some priests to accept, as they were used to respect, to being treated as if they were very important. He could get very edgy at times, too. His battle with the officials, safe and snug on the bigger islands, was making him tired and bitter. He kept up his barrage of letters to the Hawaiian government, begging them to send timber, nails, tools, anything he could use to put up proper housing. The Hawaiian government behaved as though it was stone deaf. Damien was reaching boiling point. There they sat in their comfortable offices, safe from the wind and the rain, while his people rotted away in disgusting shacks. He was just about to start another spate of letters when his problem was taken care of.

*"[Father Damien] is now 49 years old – a thick-set, strongly-built man with black curly hair and short beard, turning gray. His countenance must have been handsome, with a full, well-curved mouth and a short, straight nose; but he is now a good deal disfigured by leprosy, though not so badly as to make it anything but a pleasure to look at his bright, sensible face. His forehead is swollen and ridged, the eyebrows are gone, the nose somewhat sunk, and the ears are greatly enlarged."*
Edward Clifford,
from "Father Damien."

## The typhoon

A typhoon hit Molokai in late 1874. All night long it raged, the sea roaring and crashing against the rocks, the palm trees lashing in the fury of the wind. The people huddled together as the rotten thatch of their homes was ripped away by the gale. The ramshackle huts simply disintegrated. Morning found a wet and dejected population, but Damien was delighted. He wrote once more. This time even the officials could not say that it

37

was an unnecessary request. Of course, they grumbled and quibbled, but eventually a ship anchored and a load of timber and nails was put ashore. There were, of course, no carpenters or builders, but Damien and the villagers had repaired the church and fenced the graveyard – what were a few huts?

Many of the villagers were too sick to help, and some too lazy, but Damien had eight willing helpers. This time the houses were real houses, well made and decent places to live in. Damien saw to it that they were raised a little off the ground, so that they did not get sodden and rot. Damien and his crew built three hundred houses in the end – and now he, too, had a proper house of his own instead of a hut. It was as bare and poor, but it was dry, clean and a place people could find him if they needed him.

At first, Damien remembered what the Bishop had said and would not allow anyone with leprosy to come into his house. He did not want to catch the disease, not only for his own sake, but also because he wanted to stay healthy enough to work and to help his people. Women without the disease cooked his meals and cleaned his house – he thought it a sensible precaution.

But now he thought, "Every day I work with these people, touch them, clean their wounds, breathe the air they breathe. Every day I dig their graves and bury their dead. It's a bit silly to ban them from the house."

So the villagers who, like the healthy islanders, enjoyed a little company and conversation, used to drop in on Damien and spend a while in his room. He winced a little when they tried his pipe – but said not a word. He was as healthy and strong as ever.

## Bright days and dark days

Dirt and thirst. They still had to be tackled. The water supply on the peninsula had always been a nightmare. Whatever Damien had achieved, he knew he could not begin to make a decent life for them unless he could provide a reliable supply of clean water. And without water diseases spread and crops can't grow.

There was a source of good water, but it was too far away to be of much use, over half a mile from Kalawao. It needed to be piped to the village so he wrote to the government officers and asked for pipes. Nothing happened.

Damien chewed his pipe and wrote again. And again. And again. The government officers were sick and tired of letters from Damien and, probably to stop the flood of letters, he got his pipes and taps. Not that they sent any engineers or plumbers to help fit it all up – no engineer or plumber would have dared to go near the settlement as they would not have been allowed to leave again.

How Damien must have blessed the name of Janneke Roef. Once again, his childhood experience back in Belgium was there to help him. It certainly seems to have been of far more use to him than his Latin and Greek.

He got together the fittest, strongest men he could find and they set out to lay the pipes all the way from the distant pool to the settlement. It was hard work, hacking and digging and dragging the pipes to where they were needed, and it took months of work, but one glorious day the people gathered in the villages to see the taps turned on for the first time, and a steady stream of clear, cold, bright water gushed into their bowls. There would be no more struggling along the track to the foot of the Palis: it was another huge step forward. The pipeline was extended to Kalaupapa in 1888.

## Visitors and friends

Times were changing, even in Hawaii. Perhaps Bishop Maigret had more courage than most, or perhaps he had more sense. He and Father Albert Montitor arrived on a pastoral visit in June 1875.

Damien was as pleased as a small boy, showing them the changes he had made, the improve-

"I picture him as always ready to take up with great vigour anything that presented itself as his actual duty, and, further, anything at all that he thought would be good, whether it was actually his duty or not. Anything that appeared to him to be good – good to do – was something for immediate action; he apparently considered it really his duty. He did not give much time to the study of expediency, or the cost, or the danger."

Brother Joseph Dutton, on Father Damien, from "The Samaritans of Molokai."

*An aerial view of the church built by Damien at Kalaupapa. Most of the non-infected people on the peninsula lived in this village.*

ments, the houses, the church. The people of the two villages were delighted beyond belief. Someone had remembered them, someone important had praised their work, and their priest.

A Dr Woods came next, the Chief Medical Officer of Brooklyn Hospital in the USA. Woods had been all over the world and he told Damien this was by far and away the best settlement he had ever seen. Damien positively glowed – and his people were as pleased as he was. At last they had something to be proud of. He was still strong, still handsome, but he told the doctor that he was quite sure he would become a leprosy sufferer in the end – the risks were too great for it not to happen. Despite all this, he seemed unworried and cheerful and excited about new projects.

## New worries

If the old anxiety had lifted, new worries were on the horizon. Damien's good friend, the superintendent, had retired and, to his horror, the job was given to Damien himself. He felt he didn't have the right experience and would make a terrible mess of it. He did.

Mercifully, they soon found someone else. Unfortunately it turned out that they had made a bad mistake. Damien had got into a muddle, but at least he had *tried*. This man meant well, but he did not do enough or keep an eye on the people under him. They were a bad lot and Damien was to have endless trouble with them.

It was not until 1878 that another priest was sent to help him in his immense task. Unfortunately Damien had a very quick temper and quarreled with both this man and the priest who replaced him in 1882. Damien never lost his temper with the leprosy victims, but he just couldn't understand why all the members of his Order were not as enthusiastic and tireless as he was. Damien was definitely difficult to get on with – he was argumentative, very obstinate and disorganized. Joseph Dutton, who was later to become his willing helper, described him as "vehement and excitable in regard to matters that did not seem to him right and he sometimes said and did things that he afterwards regretted."

When the second priest left in 1885, Bishop Koeckmann refused Damien a replacement on the grounds that if he had been less quarrelsome, the other priests would not have left. Of course by 1885, Damien was suffering from leprosy himself and couldn't manage as well as he had in the past.

## Things look up

All the same, things really *were* getting better – not only had Damien found a valuable friend and helper in one of the sufferers, but a new doctor, Dr Emerson, had arrived on the island too.

Damien took to building again – this time an orphanage for the boys. He had already built one for the little girls and installed a lady to act as cook, cleaner and mother to them. Now, forty boys were safely housed, though it was years before he could get proper staff to look after them.

*"The average of deaths is about one a day. Many are so destitute that there is nothing to defray their burial expenses. They are simply wrapt in a blanket. As far as my duties allow me time, I make coffins myself for these people."*

Father Damien, in a letter to his brother, Father Pamphile, dated November 25, 1873.

41

Father Damien, surrounded by young boys from the orphanage. Sometimes children with leprosy were sent to Molokai without their parents. Often too, the parents died of leprosy leaving their infected children to cope alone.

Damien even built a school, which grew as the years went by.

Building occupied a very great part of his life. He cleaned out and repaired the abandoned hospital that had been put up long before he came to Molokai and opened it with some of the fitter girls as nurses. The new doctor brought medicines which could ease the symptoms a little, even if they could not cure the disease itself.

In 1881 came a *great* excitement. Princess-Regent Liliuokalani was coming on a visit! She was the sister of the King of the Hawaiian islands, David Kalakaua. Can you imagine the preparations – the painting, the scrubbing, the garland-making and the singing practice? Damien had by now organized a proper choir, that led the processions on feast days, and a band which played instruments given by the Bishop.

At last the Princess arrived, with her sister, the Prime Minister and all their entourage. She was completely overwhelmed by the greeting she received and by the sight that met her eyes. Among the crowd she recognized people she had known when they were fit and well. It was all too much for her. The Princess burst into tears and the Prime Minister had to make the speech.

Damien showed her some of the things that had been done and she was so impressed that when she got home she sent many things the settlement needed. On top of that, she bestowed on Damien the Order of Knight Commander of the Royal Order of Kalakaua. It sounds very grand indeed, but Damien put it at the bottom of a box and forgot about it.

The newspapers had a field day – and the important people in the Church growled a little more – but Damien did not care. He was wonderfully happy.

*An aerial view of the leprosy village at Kalawao. While he was on Molokai, Damien and his helpers built over three hundred homes for the leprosy victims. He also built a hospital for 1,000 patients plus two orphanages.*

SOUVENIR.

# ALOHA OE
(My love to you.)
# MARCH.

The Queen Kapiolani.                    The Princess Liliuokalani.

Composed and arranged by

## J. THOMAS BALDWIN.

Incorporating the popular Song "Aloha Oe"

BY THE

## Princess Liliuokalani

And performed by

### BALDWIN'S BOSTON CADET BAND

AT THE

Grand Reception given by the City of Boston to

## Queen Kapiolani and Princess Liliuokalani

May 12th 1887.

Dr Emerson, with his very high fees and difficult ways, had been a worry but now, mercifully, he left. Dr Fitch, a kind and cheerful man, took over. He and Damien became very good friends and, though he was not a Catholic, he agreed wholeheartedly with Damien that the nuns must come to the island to help with the women and children.

In those days, Catholics and Protestants often disagreed violently, but Damien was discovering that Protestants could be fine people – and Protestants who met Damien were discovering the same thing about Catholics.

## The royal visit

The royal visit must have been a very great success, for the Princess-Regent came back, and this time she brought Queen Kapiolani. The outcasts told them of all that still needed to be done. Even though the hospital had been opened, the coffin and the patient often went in the same cart! The clothing money sent by the government was totally inadequate (it would only buy one shirt and one blanket for each person) and the food was often rotten when it was landed.

The Queen was shown around by Damien. Enteritis was rife, due to bad food and water, and the Queen was very much concerned. She asked Damien very searching questions and saw to it that many things he said were needed were despatched at once. Everyone who saw the celebrations was dumbfounded by the joy and enthusiasm of the people, especially the singers and musicians – despite their crippled hands and their disfigured faces.

## Dark days

In 1883, Damien discovered, a short time after he had told the doctor how fit he was, that his feet were painful and very hot – and that small yellow spots had appeared on his back. He guessed what it meant, but he said nothing.

*Opposite:*
*A music cover showing Queen Kapiolani and Princess Liliuokalani, who composed the song "Aloha Oe."*

---

**"I desire to express to you my admiration for the heroic and disinterested service you are rendering to the most unhappy of my servants; and to pay, in some measure, a public tribute to the devotion, patience and unbounded charity, with which you give yourself to the corporal and spiritual relief of these unfortunate people, who are necessarily deprived of the affectionate care of their relations and friends."**
*Princess-Regent Liliuokalani, in a letter to Father Damien with his order, dated 1881.*

---

*Opposite:*
*A photo taken in 1889 of Father Damien showing the swellings of leprosy on both his hands and face. He was still active in this period although his voice was only a whisper. By sharing the leprosy, he felt even more united with the people who had been exiled to Molokai.*

There were more good things happening. Damien loved visitors and now more people were coming to the island to see him. They tried, as they talked to him, to find out more about the way he felt about his life, but he would not speak about himself, only about his "children," the people with leprosy. He kept his secret.

The symptoms of leprosy had faded but that had been an illusion. One evening in 1885, as he was soaking his feet in a bowl of warm water to ease their aching, he realized that it was not warm at all, but boiling. He had felt nothing.

Dr Mouritz, the settlement doctor who had arrived in 1882, and Dr Arning confirmed what he already knew – leprosy had caught up with him at last.

He told Pamphile in 1885 but, in a letter to his mother, he just said he had scalded his feet rather badly, but was almost well again.

He heard that a Japanese doctor had, in 1886, evolved a new treatment to lessen the pain and slow down the progress of the disease. He wanted to try it, but the Father Provincial wrote a letter that hurt him bitterly. It said that, if he came to Honolulu, he was to be shut in one room, for if people knew there was a "leper" in the Mission, they would keep away. If he chose to go to Kakaako, the hospital for suspected cases, he would not be allowed to celebrate Mass – the most important thing in a priest's life – because none of the other priests would use the Communion chalice and the vestments that he had used. Nor could he give Communion to anyone.

The letter ended by telling him that his wanting to go to Honolulu at all "shows us that you have neither delicate feeling, nor charity for your friends and that you think only of yourself."

This to a man whose whole life was one of charity to his friends, the leprosy sufferers of Molokai, and whose only thoughts were of them. What could be more cruel?

Damien wrote back saying that the letter had hurt him more than anything since his childhood. They were treating him as they treated his friends,

*"I cannot come to Honolulu for leprosy has attacked me. There are signs of it on my left cheek and ear, and my eyebrows are beginning to fall; I shall soon be quite disfigured. As I have no doubt of the real character of the malady, I remain calm, resigned and very happy in the midst of my people."*
Father Damien, in a letter to Bishop Koeckmann, dated 1885.

the other sufferers from the disease – as if the sickness was evil and bad and made its victims so.

His right leg was now as bad as his left, and Dr Mouritz said he simply must go to the hospital at Honolulu to try the new treatment.

The Sisters were determined to make his stay happy. Sister Antonella whitewashed a room and all the nuns donated their treasures – pictures and quilts and little statues – to make it as welcoming as they could.

It was all they could do to hide their tears when they saw how desperately ill he was – but for the first time for years he slept between clean, white sheets and had proper meals cooked for him.

He was a terrible patient, escaping from his room to comfort patients waiting to be sent to Kalawao, reassuring them by telling them of the welcome they would have. The Sisters forgave him!

Unfortunately the new treatment had no effect and he soon had to say goodbye. He returned, for the last time, to Molokai.

## Help arrives – Joseph Dutton

When he got home there was a letter waiting for him. Pamphile, who was sick himself with tuberculosis, wanted to come to Hawaii to see him. Damien's Bishop was delighted and said he would be made very welcome, but the authorities in Belgium said Pamphile could not be spared.

They never saw one another again.

From Pamphile's next letter he learned that their eighty-three year-old mother had died. Damien seemed to be at the very bottom of his life. He needed something wonderful to happen.

And it did.

In July 1886, Joseph Dutton arrived. An American born in 1843, he had fought in the Civil War and done many different jobs throughout the USA. His marriage had failed and he had decided, like Damien long before, to become a Trappist monk; but he was not happy in the life. Then one day, he read an article about Damien and the leprosy villages on Molokai.

Joseph packed his bags, took a ship and suddenly turned up at Kalawao, telling the astounded Damien that he was going to stay with him as long as he was needed, to lend a hand. He stayed over 40 years, until he died. He was a man who could almost out-work Damien, strong and kind and with a sense of fun; the sort of man Damien had needed beside him as friend and fellow worker all his time on the islands.

Damien heard that a new priest had arrived in Honolulu and asked that he could be sent out to him, but got a very strange reply: "Father Sylvester does not feel that it is his vocation to bury himself with the "lepers." He does not even consider that it would be bearable to live among the healthy Hawaiians on the other side of the Palis, on account of the isolation and loneliness. A young missionary should not be discouraged."

Damien could hardly believe his eyes.

*Aerial view of Kalaupapa village showing the church and landing stage. This village is still lived in today, although Kalawao has been abandoned.*

## More help – Mr Chapman

In 1887, amidst the continuing worries, an unexpected letter came from a Church of England vicar in London, a Mr Chapman. He praised Damien's work, offered his friendship – the thing Damien needed more than anything – and said he was collecting £500 to send out to him. He would like to have come himself, but he was too poor and too many people depended on him in London.

Damien could scarcely believe that a man could be so generous. When he had scarcely anything himself, he could find money for a stranger, half the world away. He had been brought up to be very wary of Protestants, yet here was another who was goodness and kindness itself.

When the money arrived, it was nearer £1,000 than £500. Damien was ecstatic: he would be able to buy good, serviceable clothing for all who needed them. His joy was short-lived. He was reprimanded by his Father Provincial for spending the money without consulting anyone. Of course, he should have, but to Damien, his people were far more important than rules and regulations. He often made mistakes, especially with money, but was always willing to learn. If someone pointed out, quietly and sensibly, where he had gone wrong, he would always see sense – and apologize.

Damien was very sick. However hungry he was, he felt awful the moment he ate anything. His heart was failing, his eyes growing dim, his voice fading to a whisper. His skin was horribly ulcerated and his nose damaged. The doctors were appalled to see the speed of the advance of the disease. His ears were swollen, his eyebrows falling out, his left leg very painful, but still he forced himself to go on working.

People who knew him wrote long after that, although he had been kind to the villagers before, now that he too had the disease, he became light-hearted. He played with the children and laughed and joked with the older people. It was as if he

*"I feel no repugnance when I hear the confessions of those near their end, whose wounds are full of maggots. Often, also, I scarce know how to administer Extreme Unction, when both hands and feet are nothing but raw wounds. This may give you some idea of my daily work. Picture to yourself a collection of huts with eight hundred lepers. No doctor; in fact, as there is no cure, there seems no place for a doctor's skill."*

FATHER DAMIEN

now felt he was one of them, a relative rather than their priest.

Damien had been a priest for nearly twenty-five years. That should have been a great cause for celebration but, in his gloomier moments, he felt there was little to celebrate. Three new priests had come to Honolulu, but none were to be spared for the leprosy settlement. He tried very hard not to be bitter, but he felt very hurt.

## More troubles – and Conrardy

The Franciscan Sisters he longed to have working on Molokai now wrote to Damien. They wanted to come, but they had been told that they would not be allowed to receive Communion from the hands of a "leper" and must wait until a healthy priest was living on the island.

Just as he began to feel like giving up, a priest called Lambert Conrardy arrived in Honolulu in 1888, asking to be sent to help on Molokai.

Conrardy was eager to help, but he found it all far harder than he had anticipated. He could hardly bear to eat his food, fearing that it might have been touched by someone infected.

Perhaps Damien did not think, or perhaps he was quietly teasing him when *he* passed him a plate and assured him that *this*, at any rate, had not been touched by "a leper."

Conrardy was afraid, but he tried his best not to show it. One morning a dying child lurched out of a doorway and fell at his feet and he nearly fled. Damien gathered the little boy into his arms and comforted him, saying to Conrardy, "Thank heavens we got here when we did." Poor Conrardy felt very ashamed and helped Damien, even though he could scarcely bear to touch the child. He had not yet learned to see the person and not the illness, as Damien had.

On the way back to the house, Damien told him that he had seen three consecutive colonies come and go since he had been on the island. Conrardy shuddered – and wondered how long he himself would last. But he stayed, and was one of the priests with Damien when he died.

*"Every morning, then, after my Mass, which is followed by an instruction, I go to visit the sick, half of whom are Catholics. On entering each hut, I begin by offering to hear their confession. Those who refuse this spiritual help, are not, therefore, refused temporal assistance, which is given to all without distinction."*
FATHER DAMIEN

## The Sisters arrive

Damien had had leprosy for four years, but he had what is called a "remission," which is when a disease stops getting worse for a while. Now there were a thousand people in Kalawao, so Damien had to go on building. The latest project was a proper home for the girls, built with money from a Protestant banker.

Then, at long, long last in November 1888 – the Franciscan Sisters arrived! Damien was so happy he forgot all his difficulties and disappointments. The little girls were in safe hands and would get some education too. He was feeling better, he had friends and he had helpers.

Outsiders were astonished by his cheerfulness, and the cheerfulness of everyone in the settlement. The frightened and dejected people who saw Damien arrive so long ago would scarcely have recognized the place. It was as though his own good, strong heart had brought life to the whole community.

Visitors who knew how ill he was, and expected to find him in bed, got a surprise. They were far more likely to find him astride the rooftop of his new church giving instructions. He had given a lot of thought and love to its design. It was specially planned for his people.

When the church was finished, the Sisters were invited to see it and were quite startled. It was painted very, very brightly, with riotous decorations. It was not at all like the bare white chapels they were accustomed to. It made them smile, but Damien's people thought it beautiful.

He had come a very long way since he felt worried and uneasy with the Hawaiian people. He had become part Hawaiian himself.

He had built a guest house so that visitors could live and sleep in a place untainted by leprosy. He would not go in, but sat outside when he went to visit them.

Brother James, a cheerful, young Irish-Australian, arrived to add to the growing number of friends and helpers he had about him. There were never enough, but the days were less lonely.

At Christmas the Sisters gave Damien a Meerschaum pipe – a very splendid affair that delighted him. They would sometimes walk down to his house to visit him, but they had been told that they must never eat with him. One day he was so eager to give them a cup of coffee that they simply could not refuse. When they got home, they got a scolding from the Mother Superior, but soon there was a dismal figure at the door. It was Damien. He'd come to apologize for getting them into trouble.

## An end and a beginning

Although Damien had been very ill again, he refused to take to his bed. It worried his friends terribly for at times they just could not see how he stayed on his feet. In the end, he had to have himself taken around in a little cart, but he still gave advice and encouragement in the whisper of a voice that was all that was left to him, glad to see his friends and the progress that was being made. As leprosy destroyed his body, he seemed to become even more cheerful and outgoing than

*Father Damien, photographed in March 1889 when he was very seriously ill. He had struggled to the altar every day as long as he had any strength.*

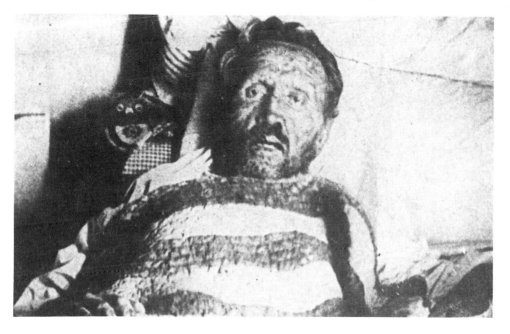

before – but he could not fight off much longer.

At long last he was forced to take to his bed, the old mattress on the floor. He did not seem sad and certainly not afraid. His friends were around him and though he still spoke of there still being so much to do he took great joy in thinking of what had already been done.

He had seen death so often in his long years on Molokai, that it was no stranger when it approached.

"Look at my hands," he said, as if he were speaking of those of one of his patients. "All the wounds are healing and the crust is turning black – that's the sign of death."

When he died on April 15, 1889, at just forty-nine, it was very quietly and gently, as if he were very tired and glad at last to sink into a long, peaceful sleep. They buried him under the pandanus tree where he had slept that first night, when he had had all the struggle before him.

Damien, that difficult, kind, good man, was dead. But all over the world people who read of him and what he had done thought far harder than they had about the scourge of leprosy. Those who were working to find a cure, or nursing those already infected with the disease, remembered him and gained courage.

## Attack and Defence

There was one more ugly thing: a Minister living in Honolulu sent a cruel letter about Damien to the Rev. H.B. Gage in Sydney, Australia, who then published it in *The Presbyterian*. It said "The simple truth is, he was a coarse, dirty man, headstrong and bigoted …" and worse.

It was a strange letter, for only four years before Damien's death the same man had written of Damien as "this noble-hearted Catholic priest who went to Molokai in 1873 to care for the spiritual welfare of those of his faith and whose work has been so successful." Perhaps, for the Rev. C. McE. Hyde, who lived in great wealth and comfort in Hawaii, Damien had been *too* successful.

*"In good Father Damien, we see one who has conquered death. He has taught the whole world such a lesson of the power of the heart and spirit of a fearless man to overcome the worst that can befall."*
Daily Telegraph, London,
April 1889.

*Damien's death spurred a worldwide effort to help leprosy sufferers. This picture shows Damien's body receiving a State Funeral in Belgium, 46 years after he died.*

But good came of it, as it so often had come from the saddest things in Damien's life. Robert Louis Stevenson, the famous poet and author of *Treasure Island*, read it and was so appalled and angry that he wrote a long letter to the press, taking every point the Minister had made and destroying it.

Dirty? "He was ... but the clean Dr Hyde was at his food in his fine house."

Head-strong? "Damien was head-strong. I believe you are right again; and I thank God for his strong head and heart."

It was a wonderful letter and made up a good deal for all the lack of understanding that Damien had had to endure.

Some of those who spoke against Damien had said "he had fallen into something of the ways and habits of a Kanaka," as if that were something

*Above:*
*A view of the leprosy village of Kalawao, from the top of the Palis of Molokai.*

*Opposite:*
*The statue of Damien by Mansol outside the Parliament Building at Honolulu. There were many complaints when it was first installed because Damien was shown suffering from leprosy.*

terrible. It was one of the best things that Damien did. He lived like the people, ate like them and he claimed no privileges because he was white and educated and a priest.

No wonder the people who wanted to look important loathed him. In their cool, clean, white clothes that they could afford, they thought to sneer at Damien's patched and shabby cassock, but all of them are forgotten now, while Damien is as loved and respected as when he died.

Nowadays, there are only a few leprosy sufferers on the peninsula and there are fewer who can remember the days before the wonder-drugs came. The little church of St Philomena on Molokai is a place for tourists to visit now. But something of the old Molokai lingers like a ghost in the air of the peninsula, as if all who lived and died there are begging visitors never to forget.

Damien's statue, outside the Parliament Building in Honolulu, is still bright with flower garlands.

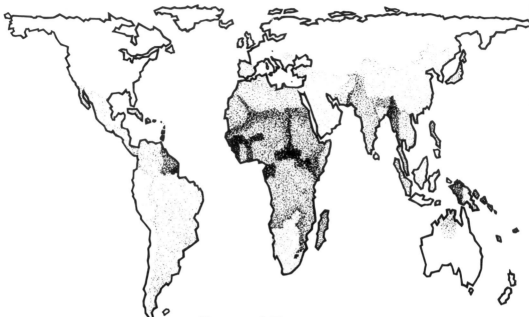

## Facts and Figures: Leprosy Today

Nowadays leprosy occurs mainly in the poorest countries. Living conditions make both discovery and treatment difficult. This computer simulation by LEPRA shows the number and location of victims worldwide – more dots show more sufferers.

Leprosy is still a major problem in many parts of Africa, South America and Asia, and one of the reasons for this is the same today as it was in Damien's day – fear.

When Damien was alive, the fear was understandable. There was no known cure, and the effects of leprosy were, as they still are, horrifying. There are two main forms of the disease – tuberculoid and lepromatous – and the disease takes a different course depending on which form the patient has. The body reacts vigorously to the tuberculoid germ or bacillus, causing irritation and whitish patches on the skin. Sometimes this form of the disease is mild, and even cures itself. About 75% of leprosy sufferers have this sort of leprosy. But with the lepromatous bacillus, which is more infectious, the body doesn't seem to put up much of a fight, so very often no symptoms appear to begin with – even though the germs are multiplying rapidly. This means that the patient can be walking around possibly infecting others, and by the time it is diagnosed, the disease has a much more serious grip on the body.

Whatever form is present, two main kinds of symptoms eventually emerge, affecting the skin and the nerves. The skin develops white patches and then massive, ugly-looking lumpy nodules appear. At the same time, the bacillus attacks the nervous system, and the victim loses all feeling in some parts of the body. If patients cut their hands or scald their fingers, or if they develop sores, they feel no pain, and so can do terrible damage to themselves. And because the bacillus seems to prefer body tissue that is cool, the hands, feet, nose and ears are most liable to attack, leading to appalling disfiguration.

People used to think that leprosy was extremely contagious, and this was another reason for fear. "Lepers" as they were called (nobody uses the word now) were shunned and driven out of towns to live on their own in isolated colonies. We now know that this is unnecessary. Healthy people with reasonable standards of hygiene very rarely catch the disease. Doctors, nurses and voluntary workers move among leprosy patients all the time without fear. Of the thousands of medical workers and missionaries who have worked with patients in the last hundred years, Father Damien is the only one to die from such contact.

Today, there are drugs that can help. We know the disease is slow to spread. And even when serious damage and ugly disfiguration does take place, the wonders of modern plastic surgery can very often help to restore something like normal features, as you will see on these pages.

The first search for a cure for leprosy started in 1847, when two Norwegian scientists published a medical atlas showing just where leprosy existed in the world. Twenty-seven years later another Norwegian, Dr Hansen, at last isolated the bacilli of the disease under the microscope. His theories were laughed at, but the long road to treatment and a cure had started. In the 1940s, a new wonder drug, Dapsone, became known, and leprosy workers all over the world breathed a sigh of relief. At last, they thought, the disease would be conquered.

But it was not to be so easy. To conquer the disease with Dapsone, patients need to be absolutely regular in taking their doses of the drug. Poor and illiterate people often do not

Mesaan Manokwari of Java. His face shows the typical swelling of leprosy and, even though he is only 14 years old, he looks like a middle-aged man. Leprosy affects the skin over the whole body. Later the swellings ulcerate and can become infected.

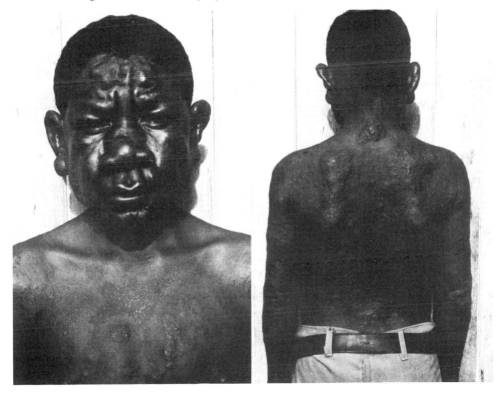

*Opposite: If leprosy is not treated, the sufferers lose fingers and toes. Often leprosy victims need to be taught a new profession as they cannot do what they used to. Here an African is learning to weave mats.*

<u>Leprosy is not highly infectious</u> *and it is not inherited. It can also be cured and the effects are minimal, provided it is discovered and treated early enough.*

understand this. They either do not know they have the disease, or they take the first pills, and when the whitish skin patches on their bodies disappear they think they are cured. So they stop taking the pills. They go back to their remote villages, and the bacilli, almost but not quite knocked out by the drug, start to fight back, and in doing so develop an immunity against further doses. So when the disease breaks out again – as it almost inevitably does in these circumstances – it is far, far harder to treat.

Recently, two more even stronger drugs have been added to the doctor's weapons. Clofazimine and Rifampicin, used in a multiple attack on the disease, are quickly curing victims – but only where the doctors have strict control over the treatment.

Nobody knows, even now, exactly how you catch leprosy; we do know that it is not quickly or easily caught, but every year, even in wealthy western countries, a few people come down with leprosy, picked up from their travels.

Of course, it is in the poorer countries that leprosy really flourishes. There are four million cases in India, and there are at least 15 million people who have the disease worldwide. Although leprosy kills, because it is so slow acting and usually confined to the poor, it does not feature very highly in medical priorities. In India, for instance, medical students have only the shortest briefing about the disease, despite the high incidence. One expert describes the problem as being "like trying to play marbles in the mud."

It seems tragic, but it looks as though this cruel, disfiguring disease is going to be with us for a long time yet.

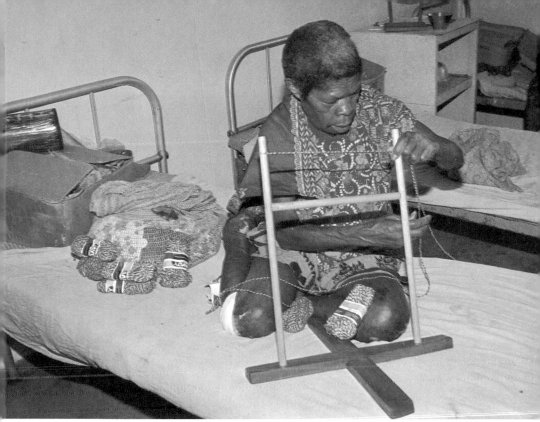

## Important Dates

| | |
|---|---|
| 1840 | Jan 3: Damien is born Joseph de Veuster-Wouters in Belgium. |
| 1859 | Joins the Picpus Fathers as a novice, and takes name of Damien. |
| 1863 | Oct 30: Sails from Bremerhaven in Germany for Hawaii. |
| 1864 | Mar: Arrives at Honolulu. Ordained a priest in May and arrives at his mission in Puna district on Hawaii Island in late July. |
| 1865 | Mar: Moves to Kohala parish on Hawaii Island. |
| 1873 | May 11: Damien arrives on Kalaupapa peninsula. |
| 1874 | Dr. Karl Hansen isolates leprosy bacillus in Norway. |
| 1881 | Princess Liliuokalani bestows Order of Kalakaua on Damien. |
| 1883 | Damien begins to suspect that he has contracted leprosy. |
| 1885 | Infection is confirmed by Dr. Arning. |
| 1889 | Apr 15: Damien dies. |
| 1908 | Dapsone is discovered in Germany. |
| 1934 | Damien's body is returned to Belgium for State Funeral. |
| 1948 | Dapsone is first used extensively against leprosy. |

*Before:* The patient has ulceration on the face and his open wounds are likely to become infected.

*Below:*
Unfortunately the early symptoms of leprosy are often not noticed. At Lulmali Leper Hospital, a doctor examines a child whose mother had leprosy.

# Glossary

**Atoll:** A circular coral reef or a string of coral islands surrounding a lagoon.

**Bacillus:** A rod-shaped bacteria.

**Catholic, Roman:** A member of the Christian community which follows the rule of the Pope in Rome.

**Conch shell:** A large and brightly-coloured spiral shell.

**Contagious:** A contagious disease is one that is spread by touching an affected person. (See *Infectious*)

**Flemish:** The language spoken by most of the people who live in northern Belgium.

**Hawaii:** A group of over twenty islands in the north Pacific, which is the fiftieth state of the U.S.A. Hawaii is also the name of the largest island in the group.

**Infectious:** An infectious disease is one that is spread through the air or in water, food, etc. (See *Contagious*)

**Kanaka:** The language spoken by native Hawaiians before the Europeans came.

**Lay Brother:** A member of a religious order who is not a priest.

**Leper:** The old name for a person suffering from *leprosy*. It is no longer used because of its association with rejection of the victim by society.

**Leprosy:** Also called "Hansen's Disease"; a mildly-*infectious* disease, mostly found in the tropics. Its symptoms include white patches on the skin and loss of feeling in face, hands and feet.

**Missionary:** A person sent to do religious or charitable work in a foreign country.

**Monastery:** A place where monks or nuns live in seclusion.

**Mule:** The offspring of a male donkey and a female horse.

**Nodule:** A lump which appears under the skin of leprosy sufferers.

**Palis:** The cliffs which cut off Kalaupapa *peninsula* from the rest of Molokai.

**Pandanus:** Also called the Screw Pine, this tree has long fibrous roots which raise the trunk three or four feet above ground level, thus forming a cave.

**Peninsula:** A piece of land that is almost totally surrounded by water except at one point where it is connected to the main part of the land mass.

**Picpus Fathers:** The Fathers of the Sacred Hearts of Jesus and Mary, otherwise known as the Sacred Heart Fathers. Damien joined the Picpus Fathers in 1859.

**Protestant:** A member of any Christian church that does not acknowledge the authority of the Pope.

**Remission:** A temporary period during the course of a disease when the symptoms decrease or disappear and the patient makes a part or sometimes complete recovery.

**Sweet Potato:** A fleshy root vegetable.

**Tuberculosis:** An *infectious* disease caused by a *bacillus* which usually attacks the lungs. Fatal in Damien's day, it can now be cured by modern drugs.

**Typhus:** A very *infectious* fever; the symptoms are a high temperature, a skin rash and a bad headache.

**Typhoon:** A violent tropical storm where winds can gust up to 200 mph. This is the name used in the Pacific; in the Atlantic they are usually called hurricanes.

*After:* This is the same young man, feeling cheerful and looking years younger.

*Below:*
*An operation to rearrange the tendons of four fingers to restore movement to the partially paralysed hand of a cured leprosy patient.*

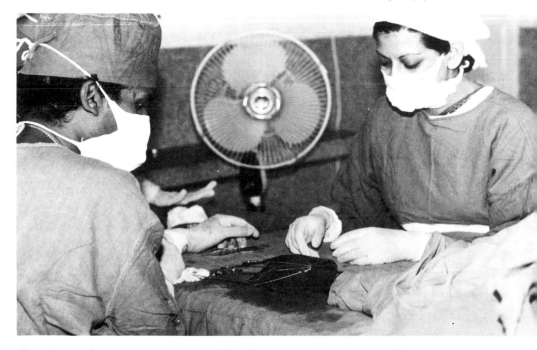

# Index

For more information about the fight against leprosy, look in your phone book for a local branch or write to a national organization, enclosing a large stamped addressed envelope. Some useful addresses follow:

**GREAT BRITAIN**
The Leprosy Mission
50 Portland Place
London W1N 3DG

**LEPRA**
105 Farringdon Road
London EC1R 3BT

**EIRE**
The Leprosy Mission
20 Lincoln Place
Dublin 2

**WORLD**
World Health Authority
Avenue Appia
1211 Geneva 27
Switzerland

**UNITED STATES**
American Leprosy Mission Inc
One The Broadway
Elmwood Park
New Jersey 07407

**AUSTRALIA**
The Leprosy Mission
174 Collins Street
Melbourne
Victoria 3000

**CANADA**
The Leprosy Mission
Suite 1128
67 Yonge Street
Toronto M5E 1J8

**NEW ZEALAND**
The Leprosy Mission
43-45 Mount Eden Road
Auckland 3